Creative Patterns 3

Coloring Books For Adults Vol.3

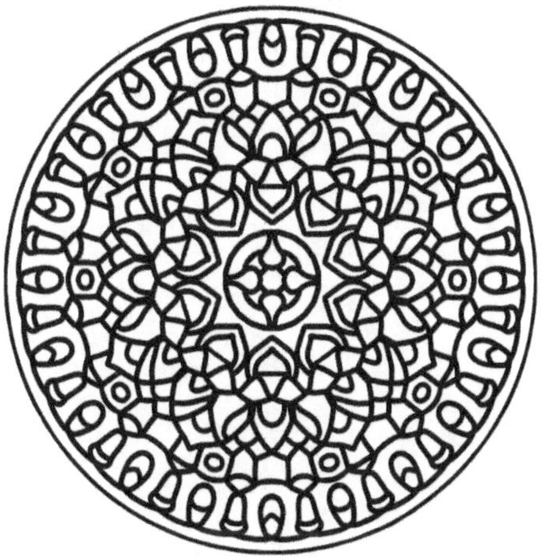
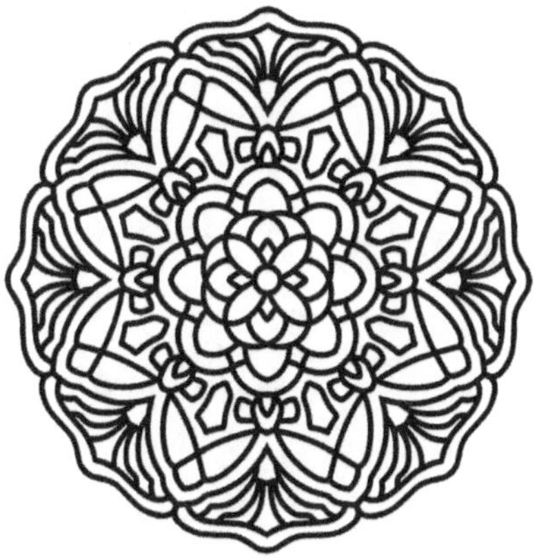

Karim Benyagoub

ISBN-10: 1508654441

ISBN-13: 978-1508654445

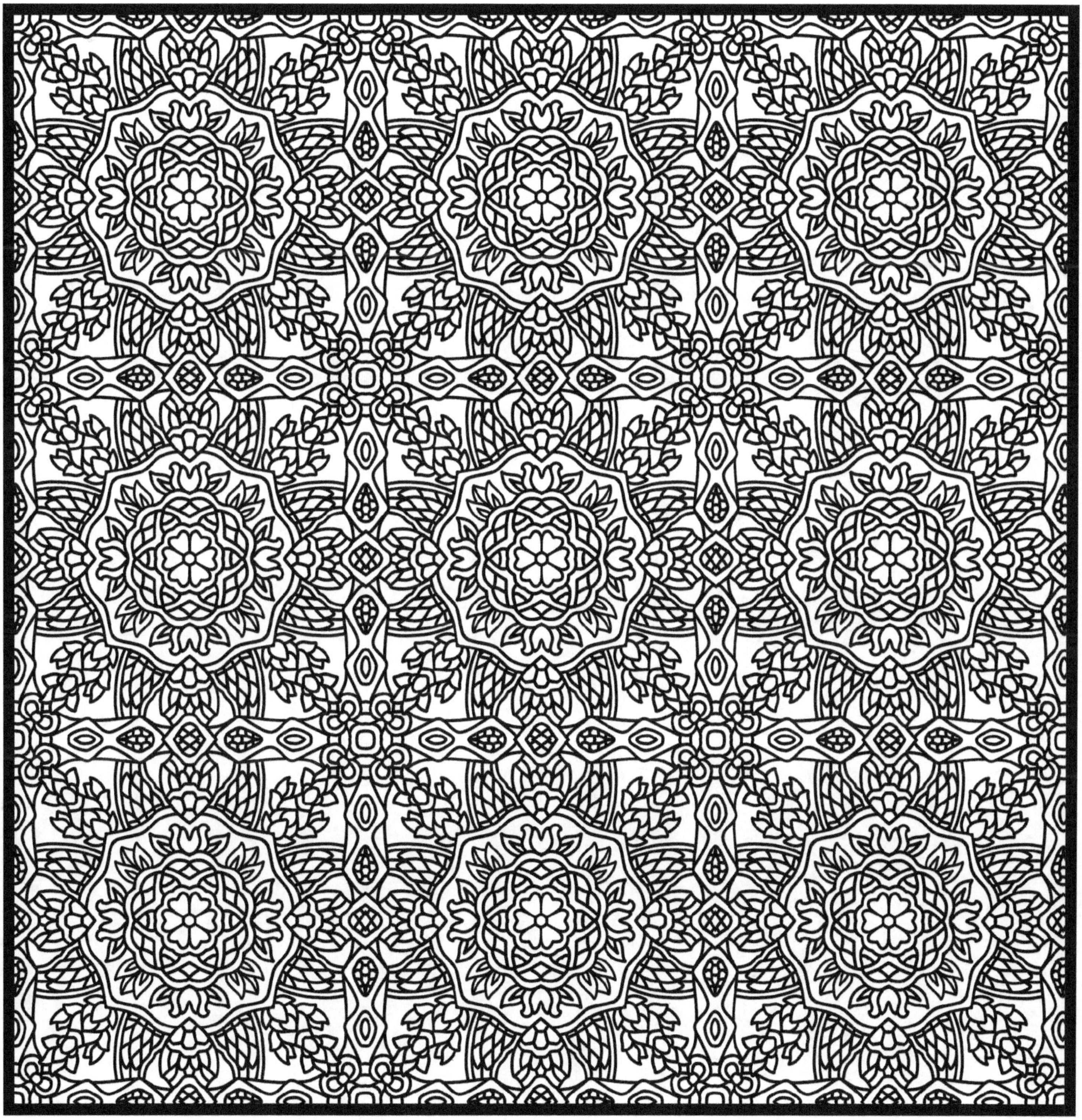

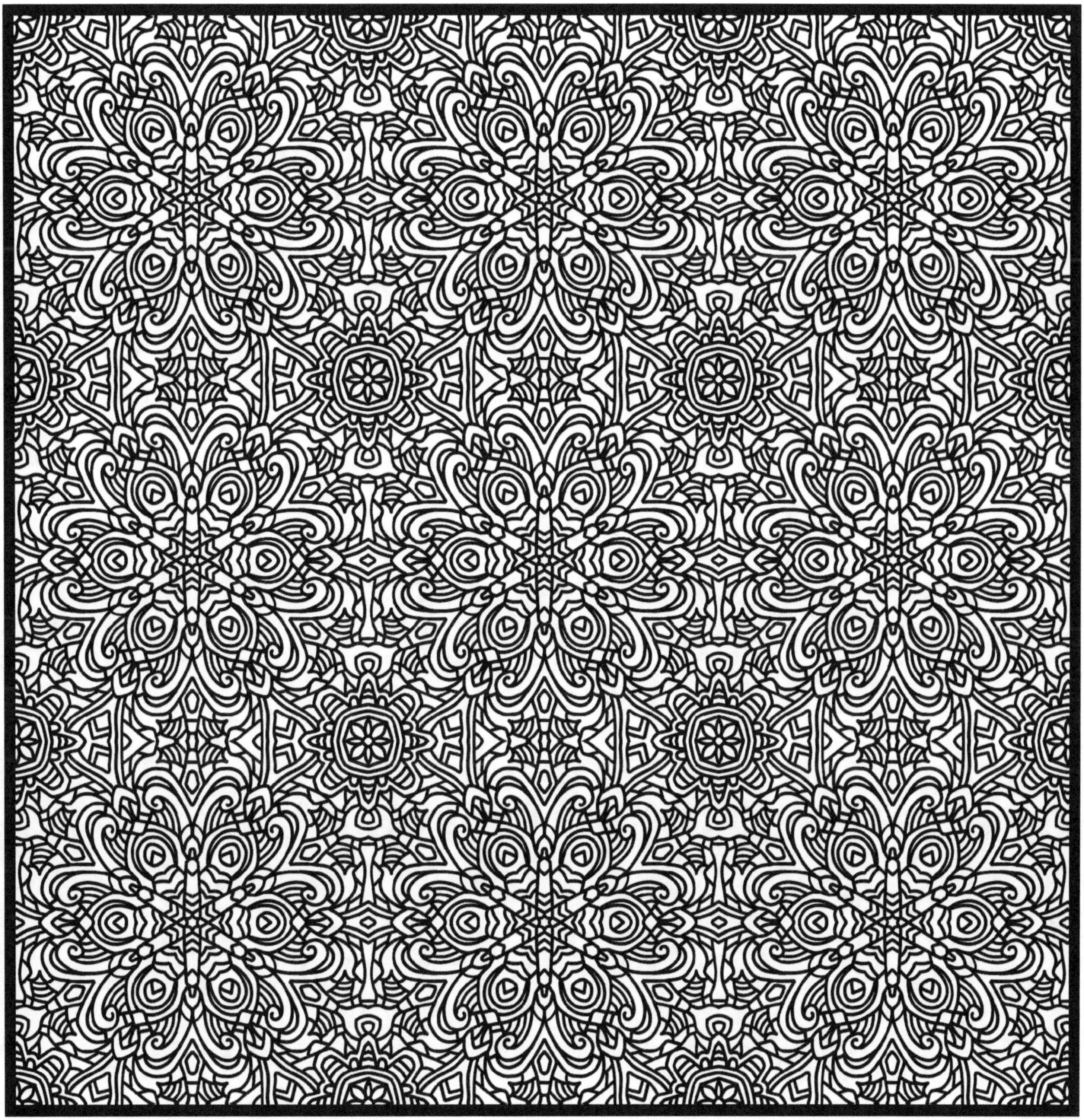

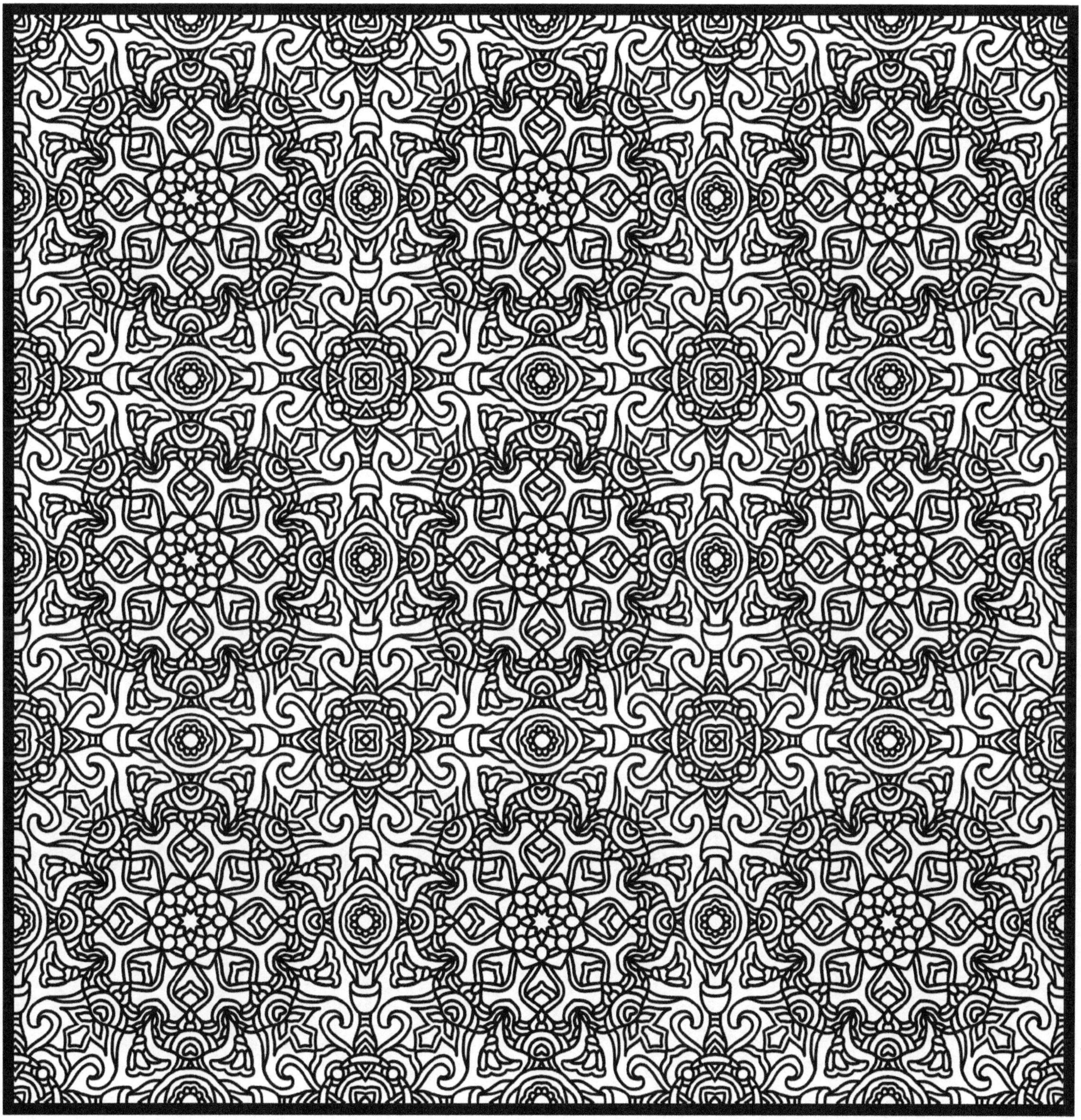

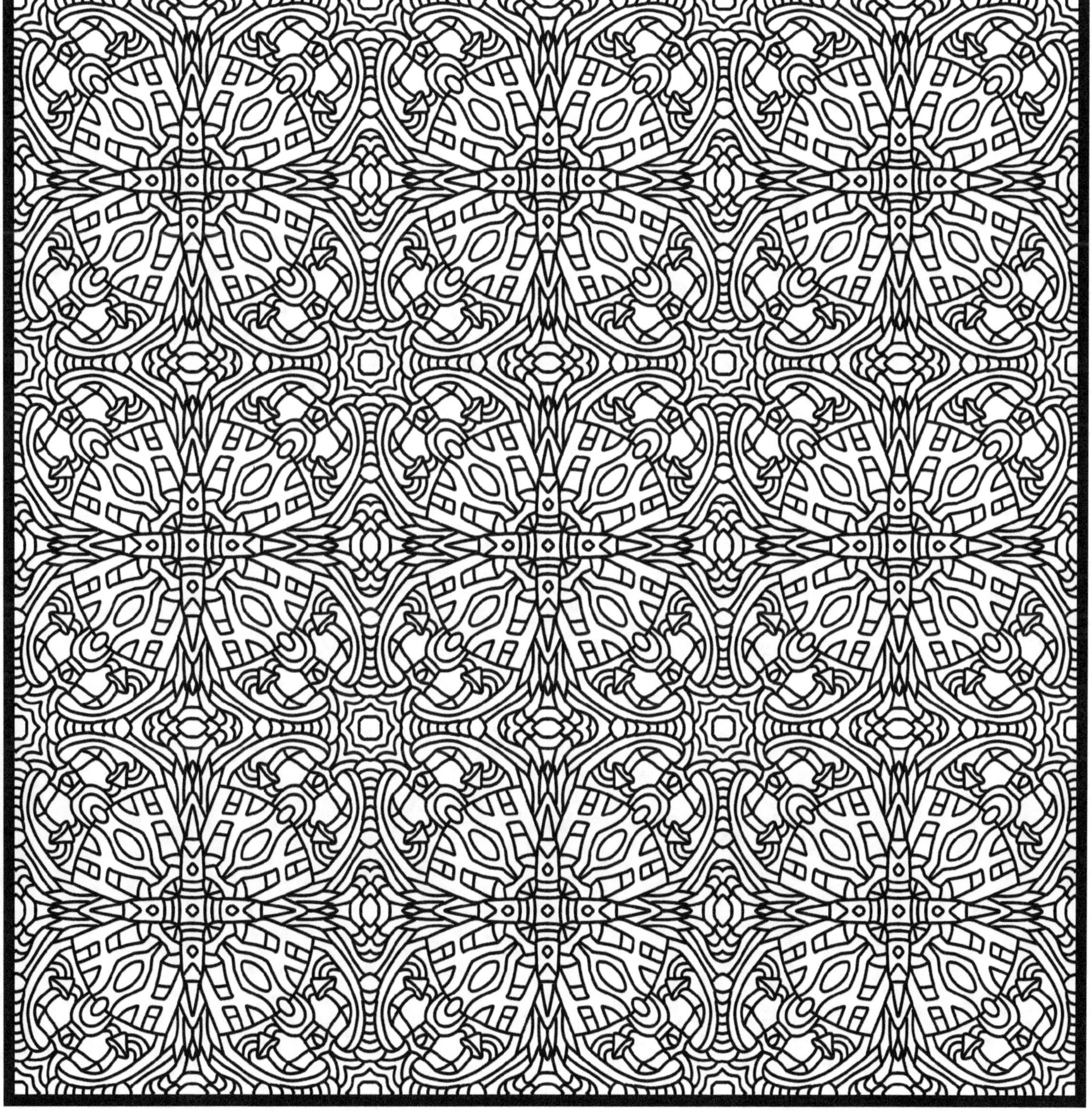

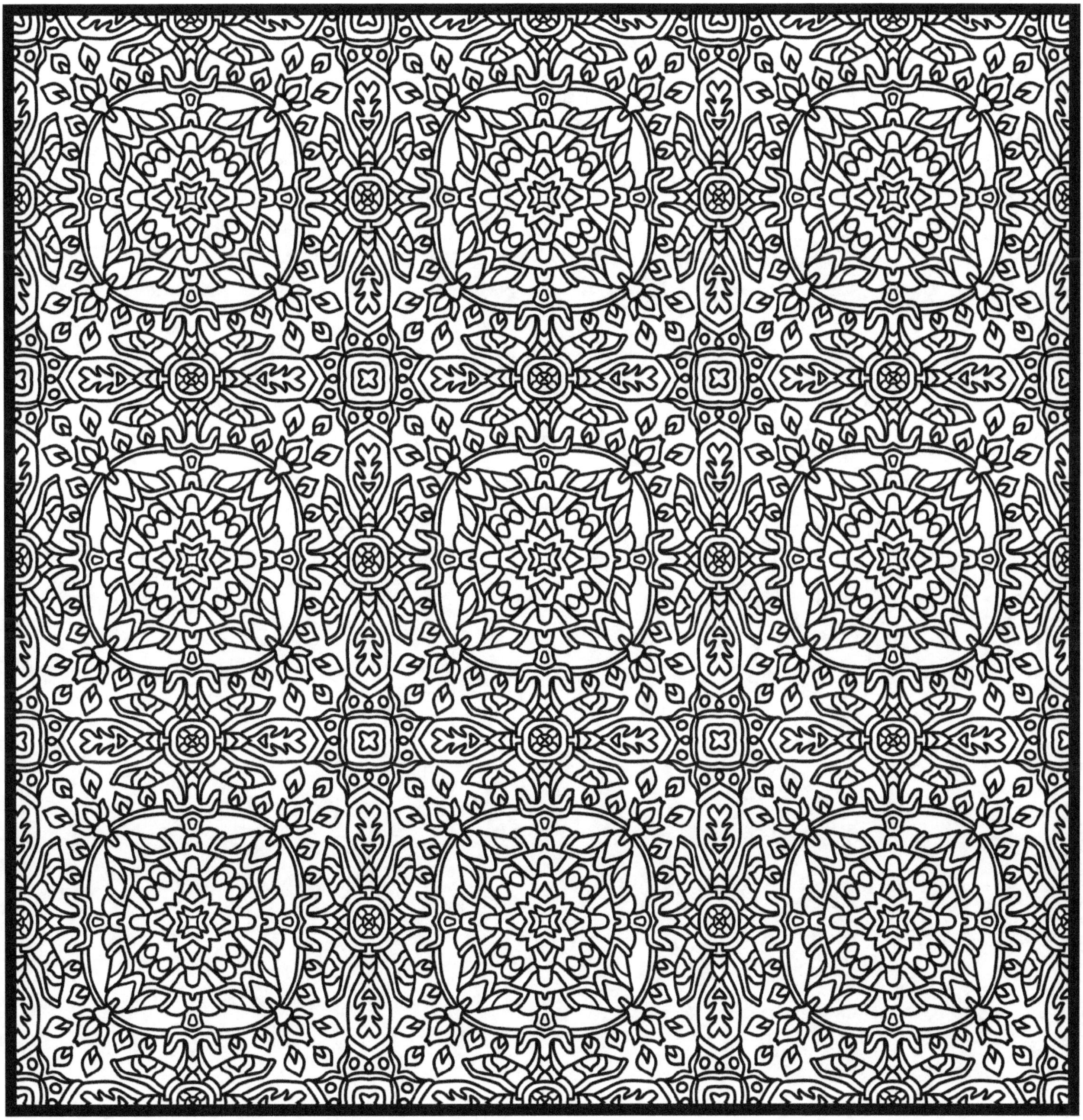

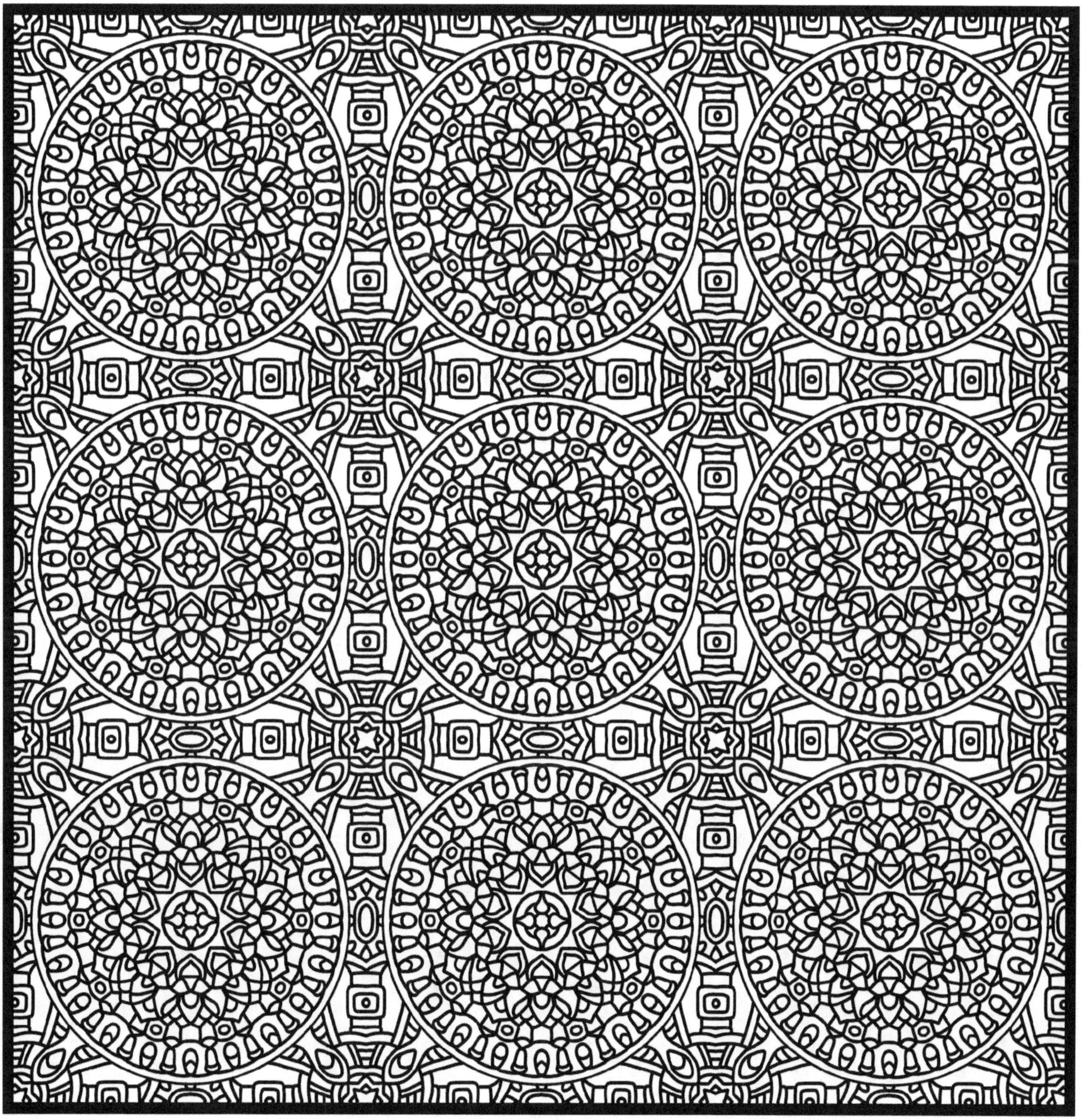

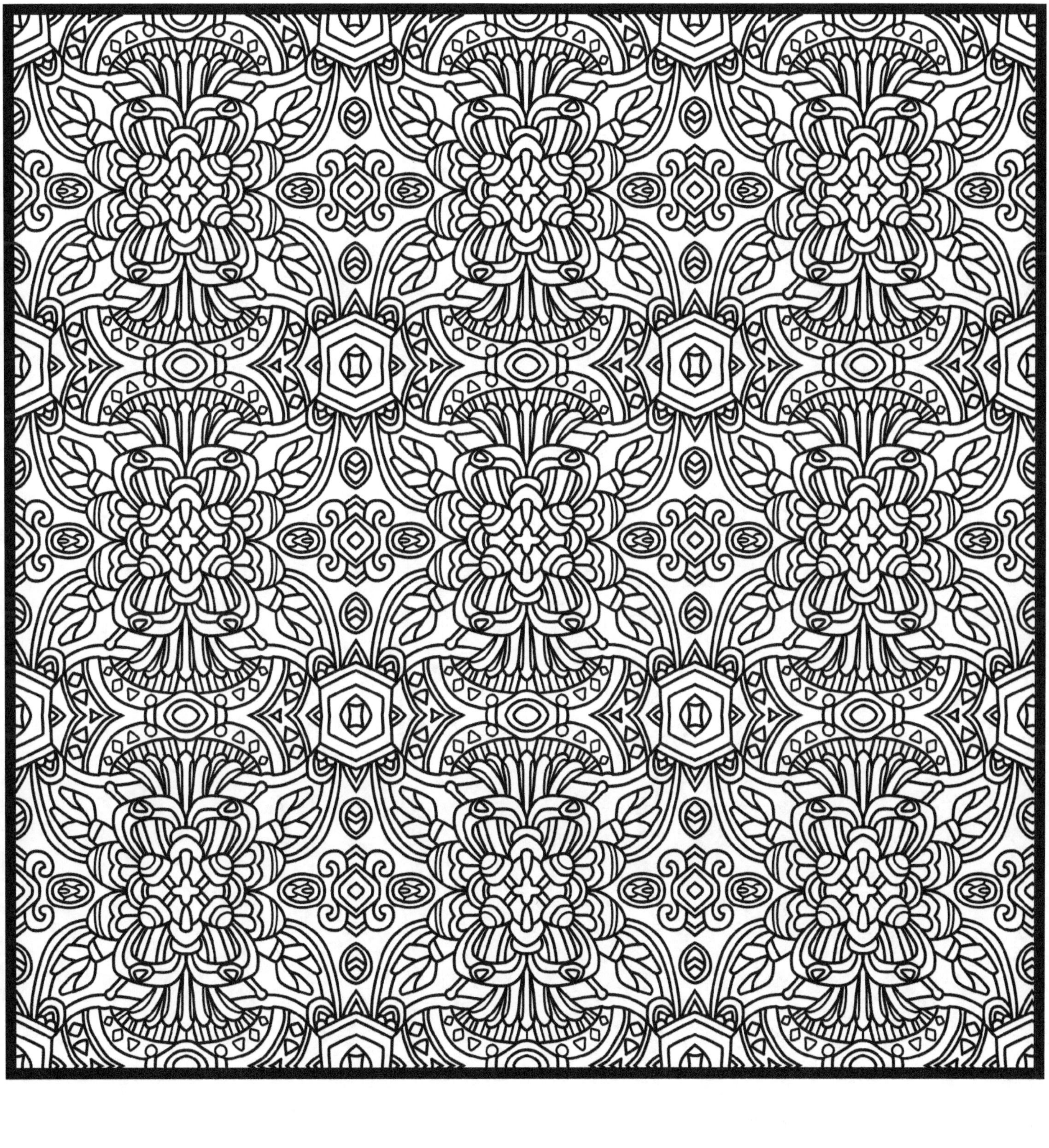

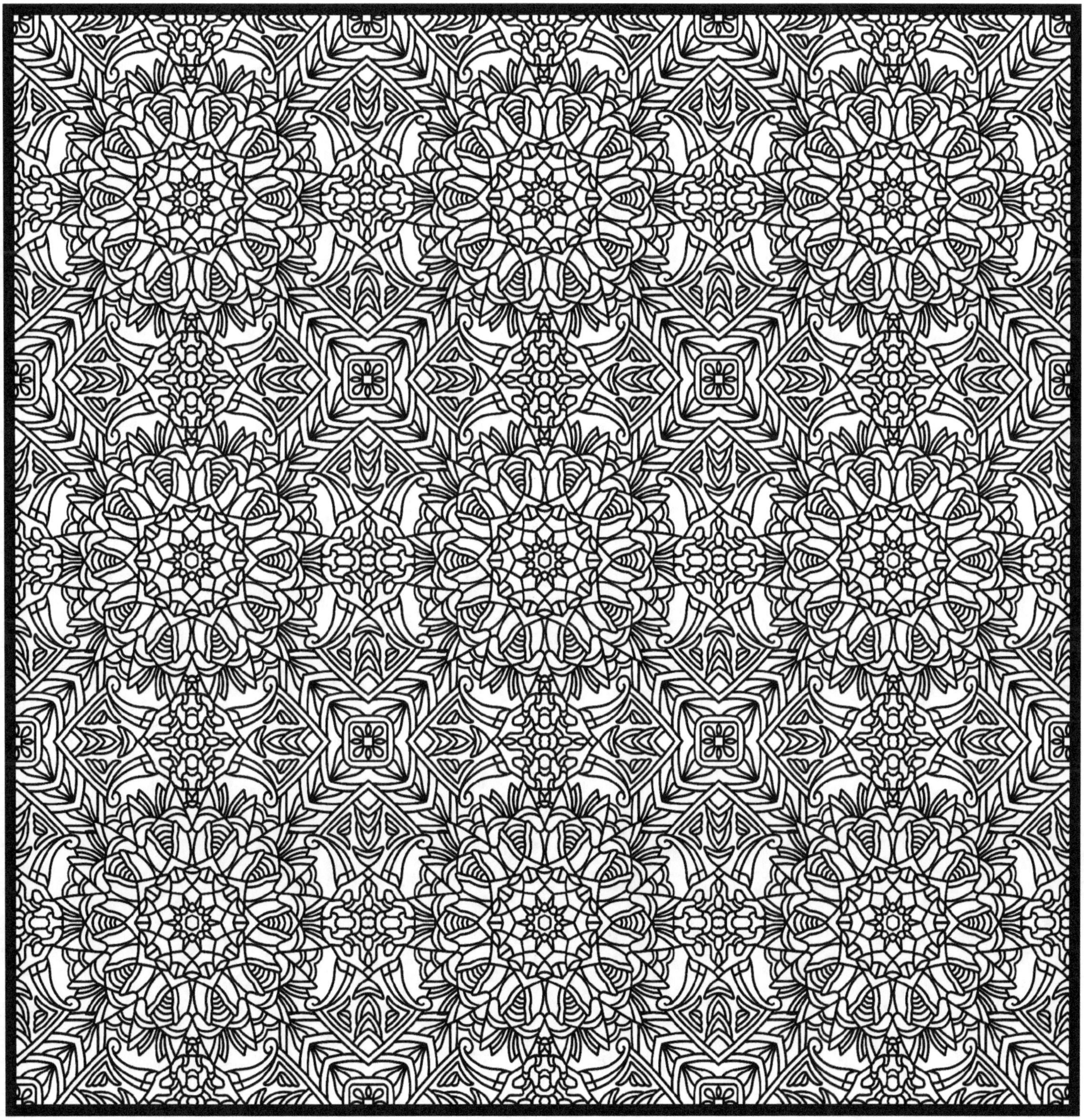

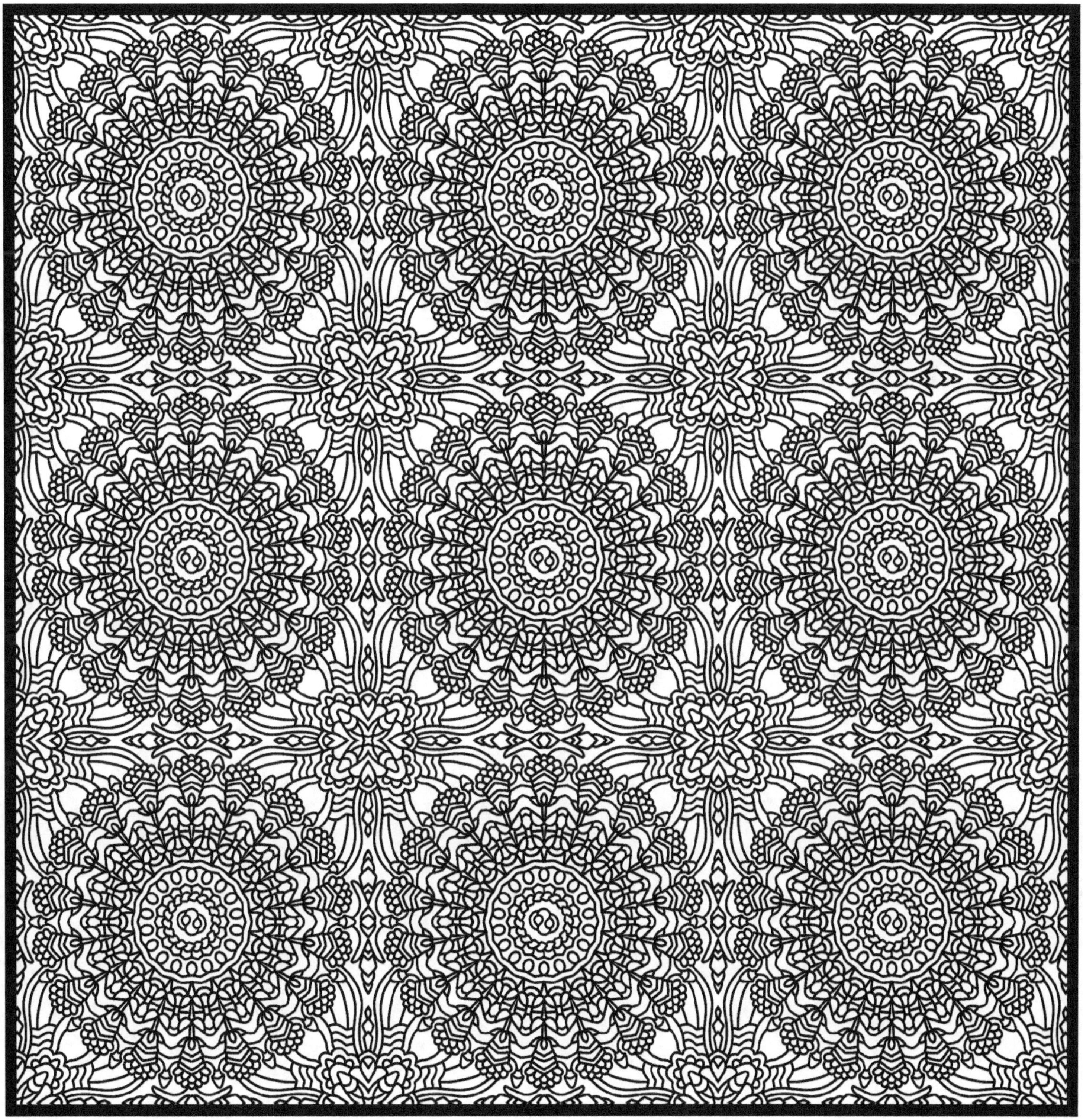

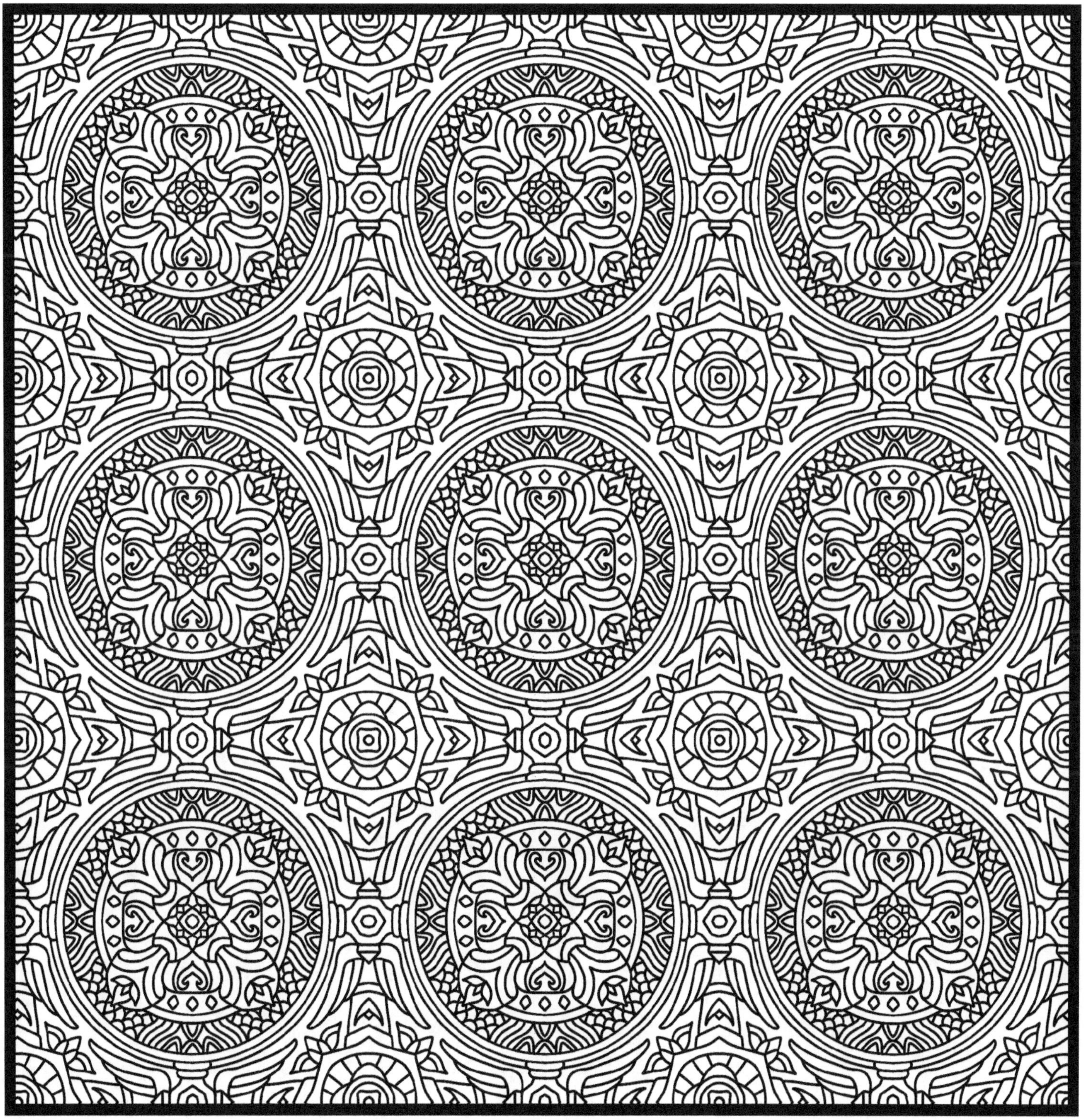

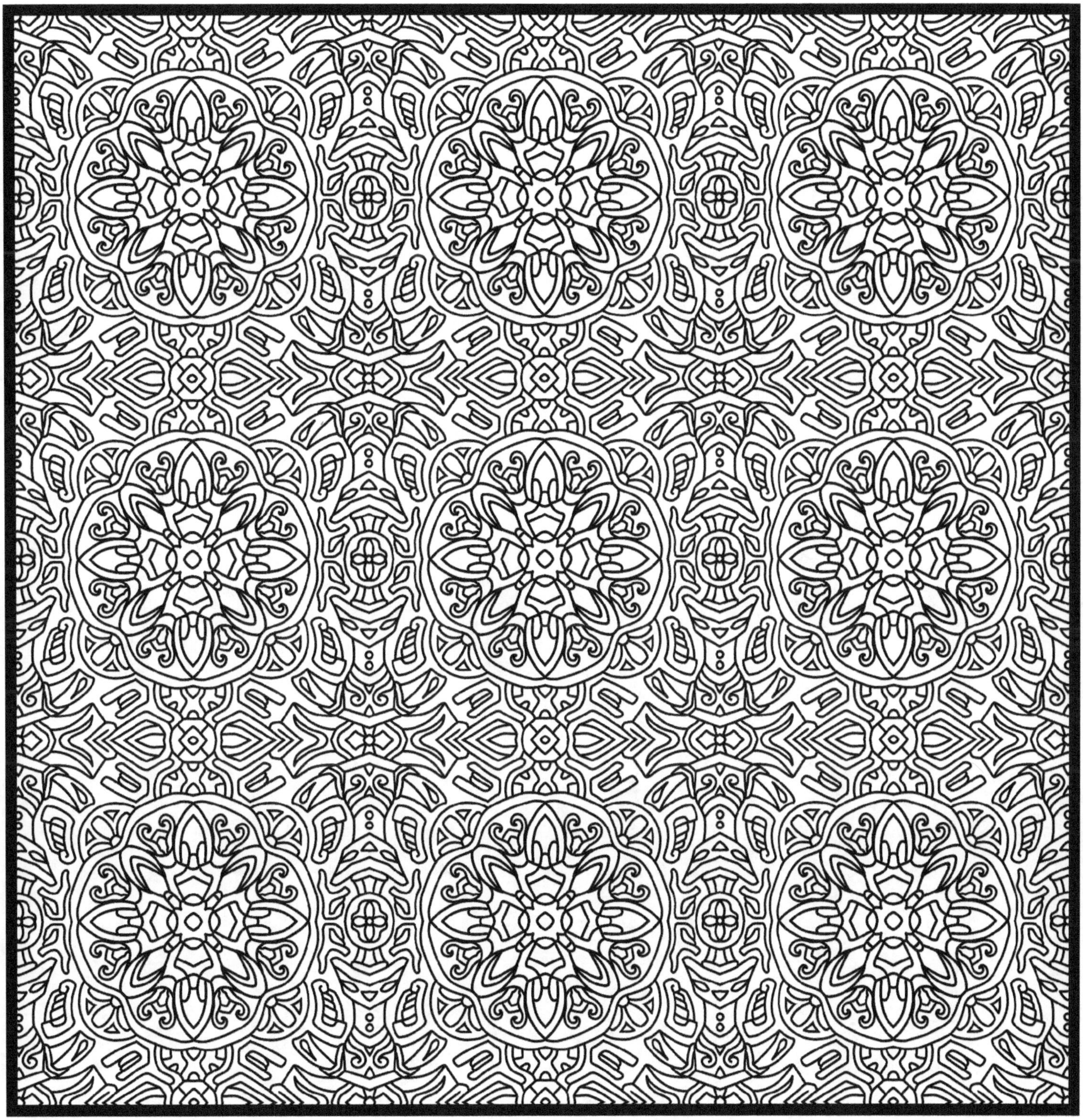

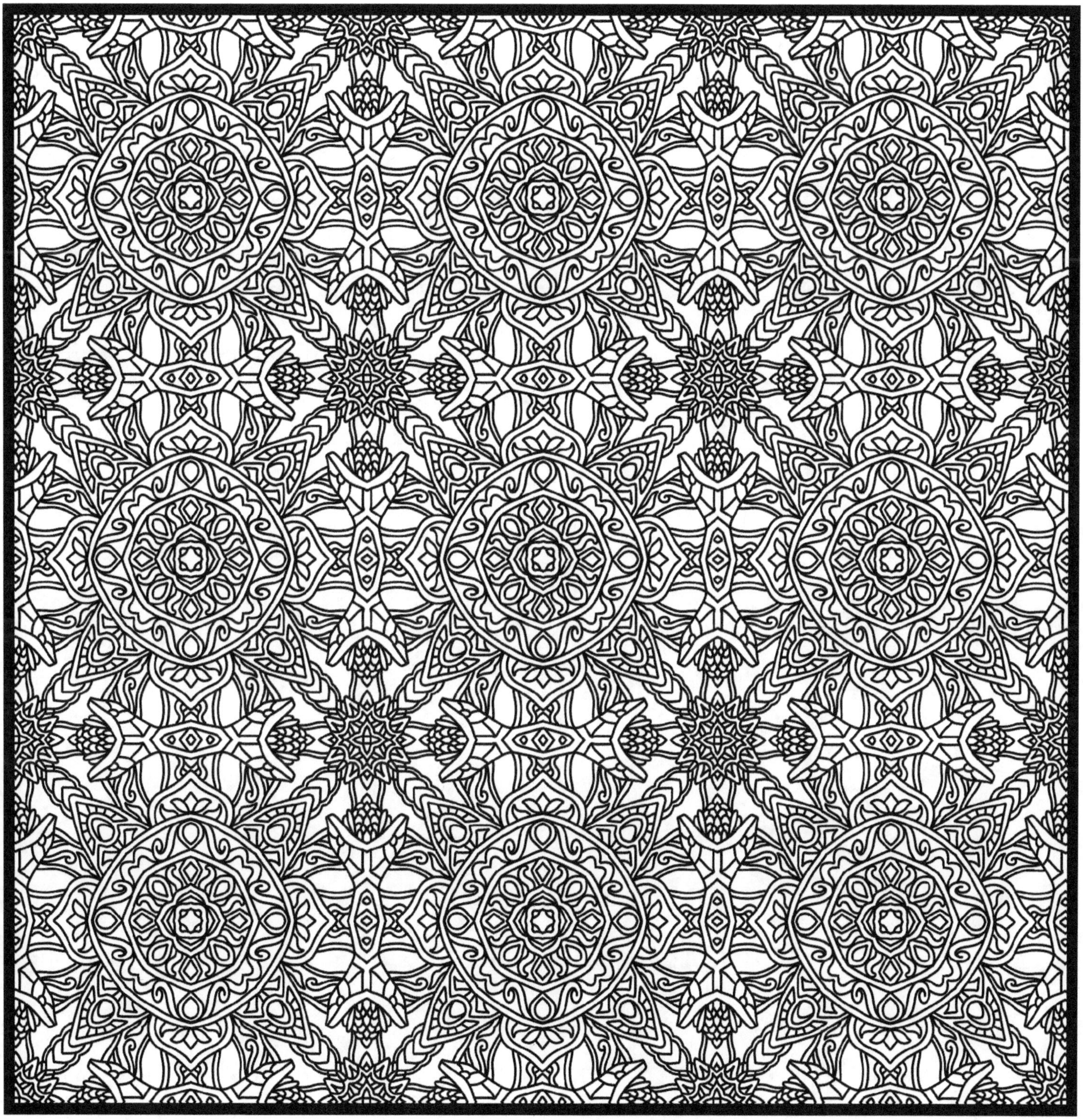

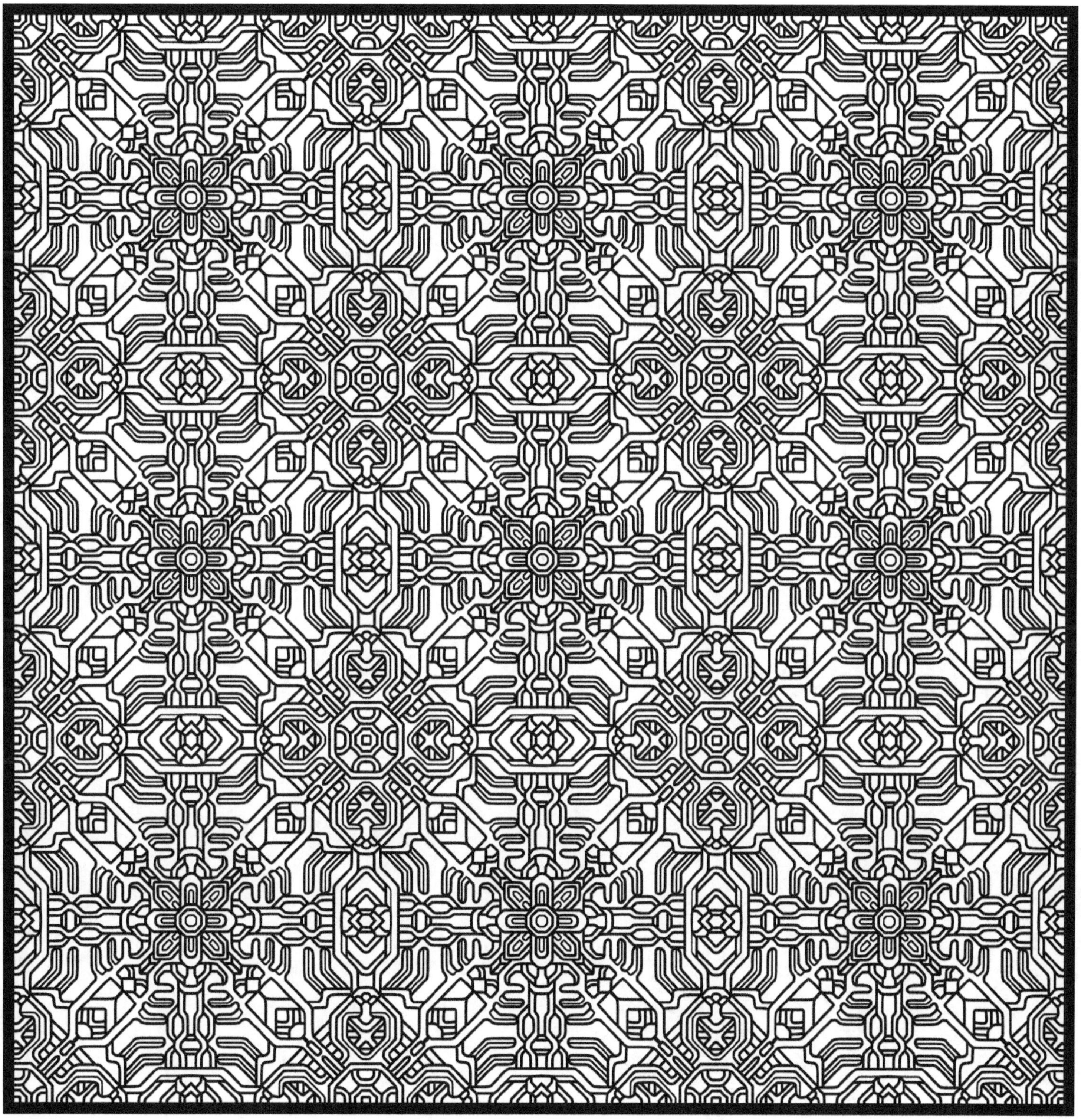

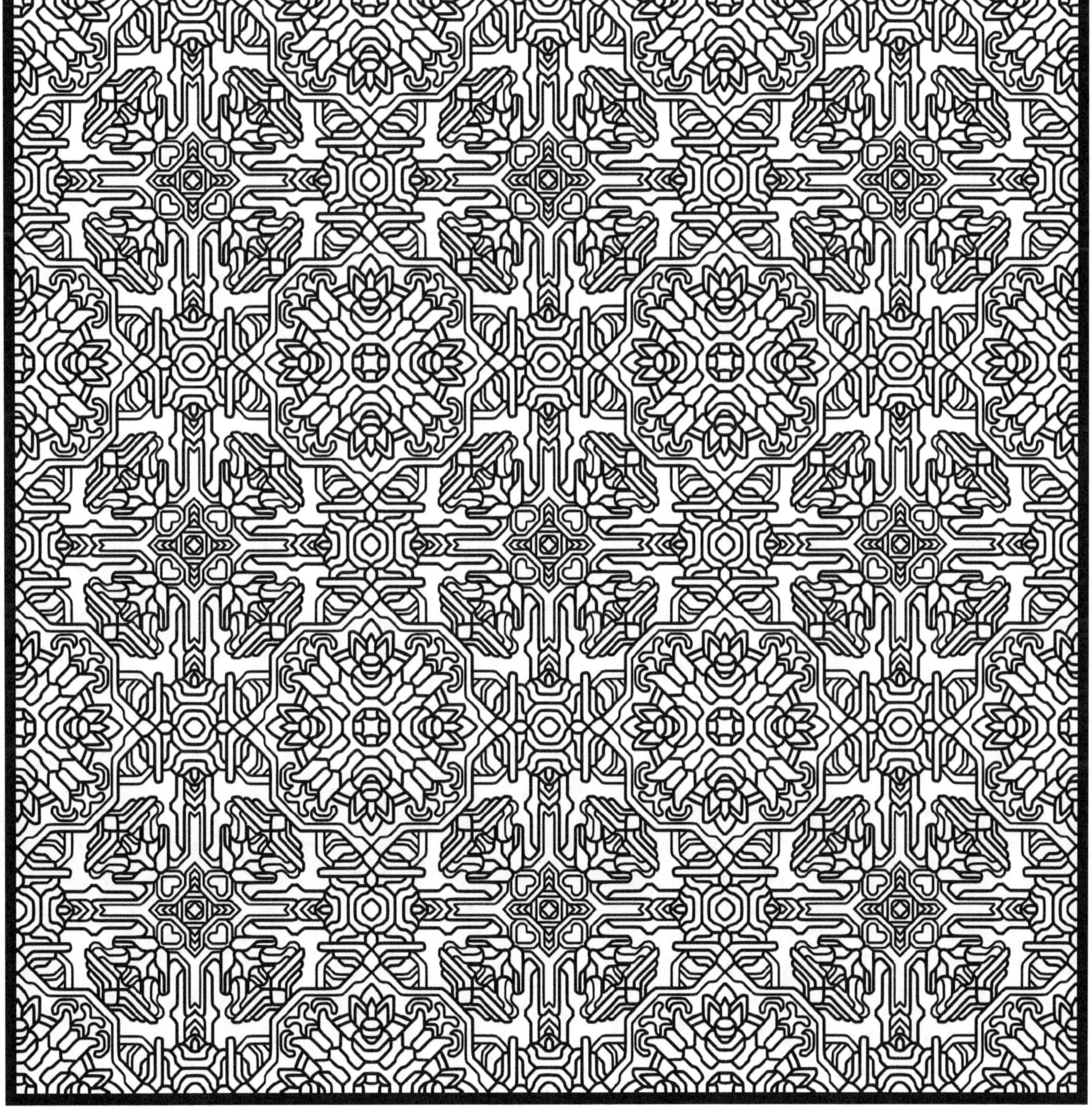

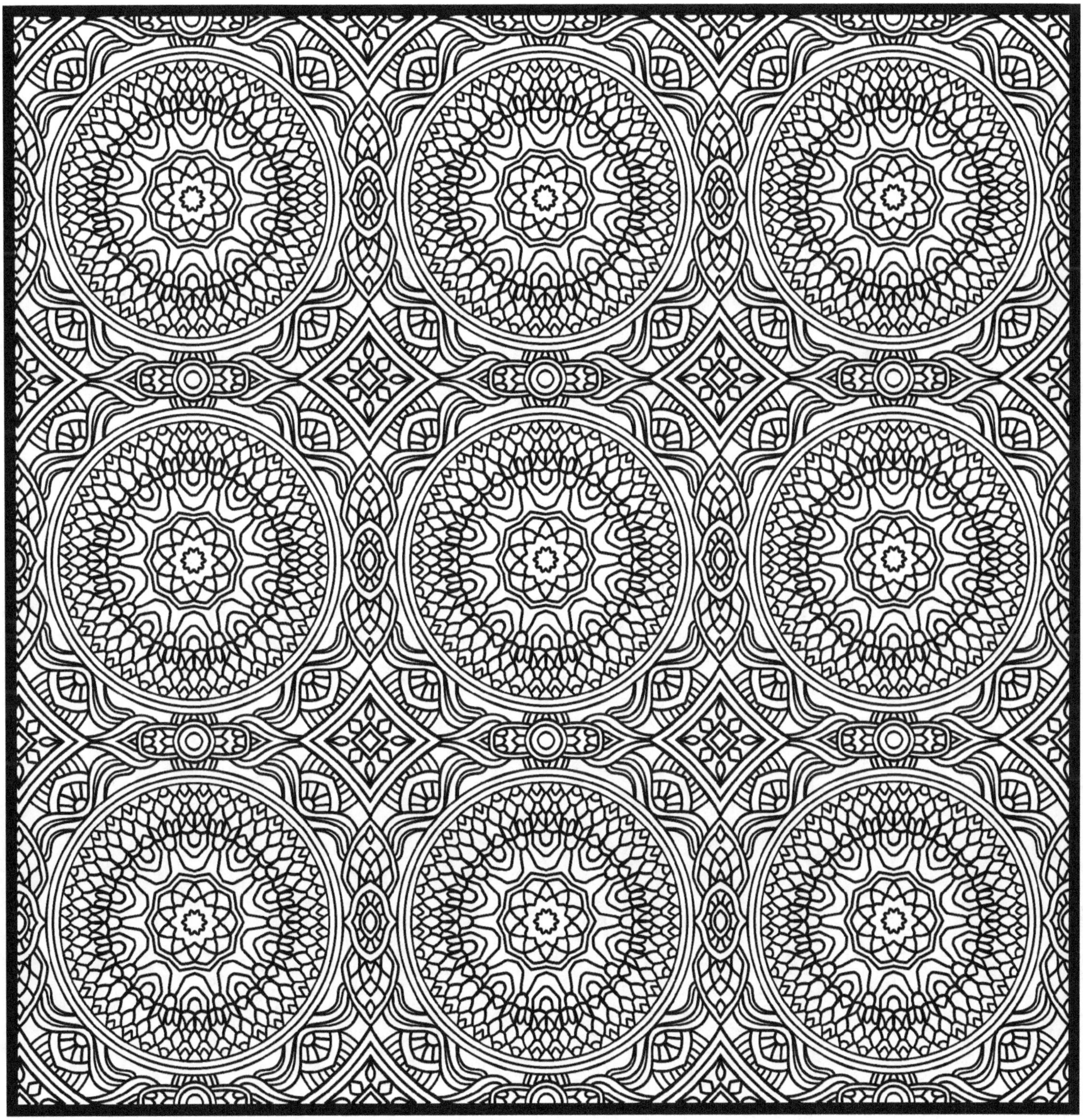

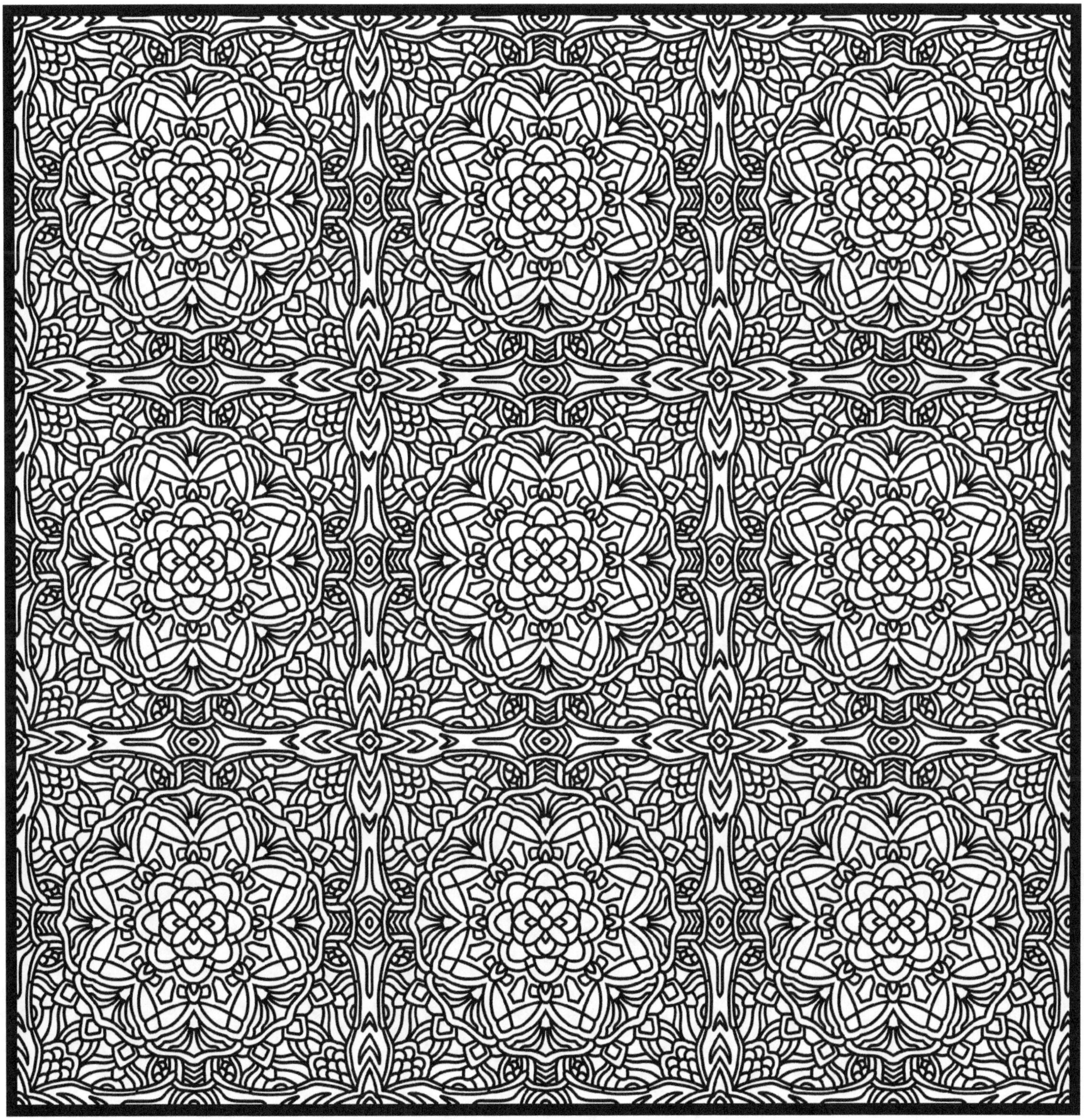

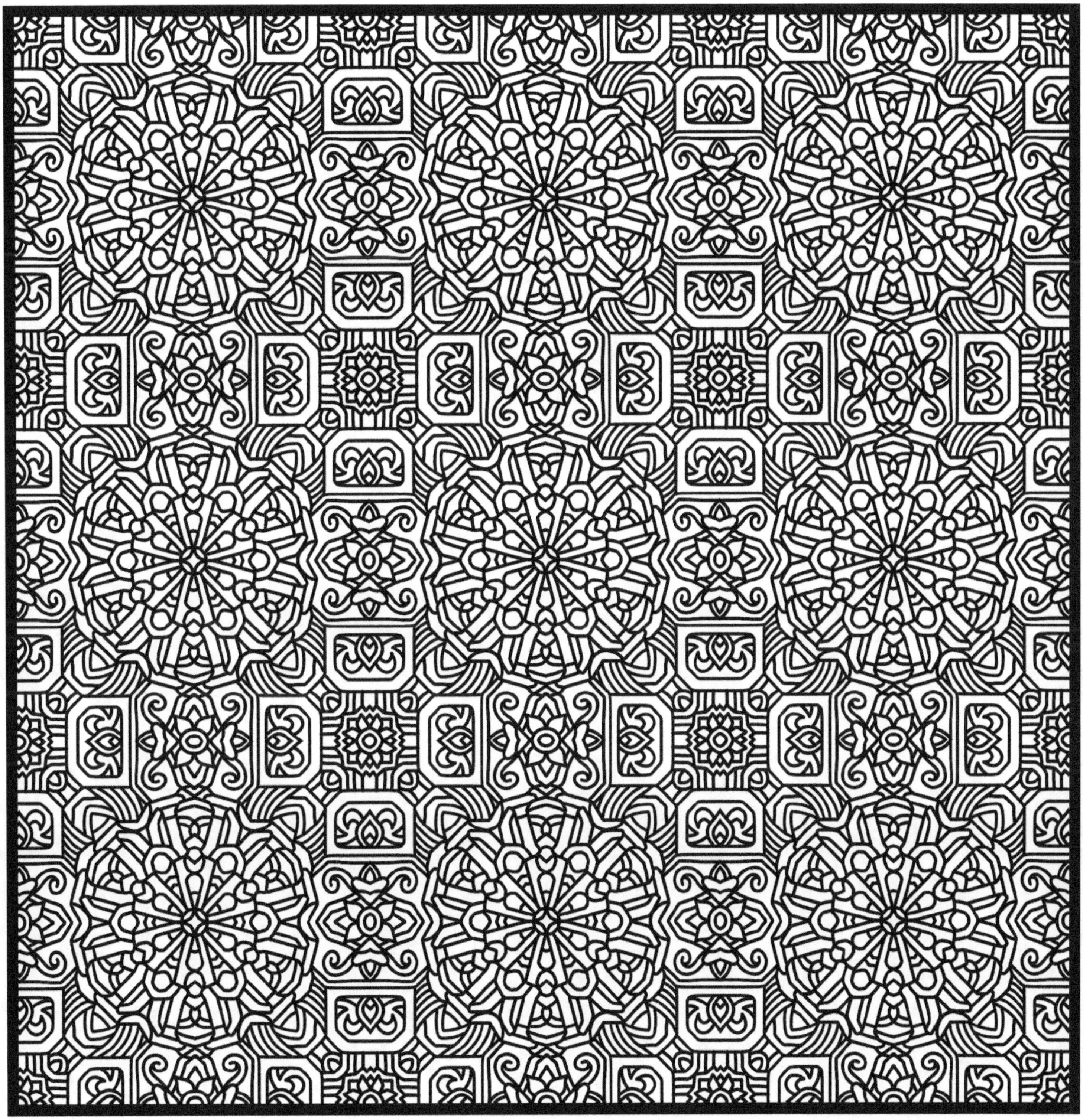

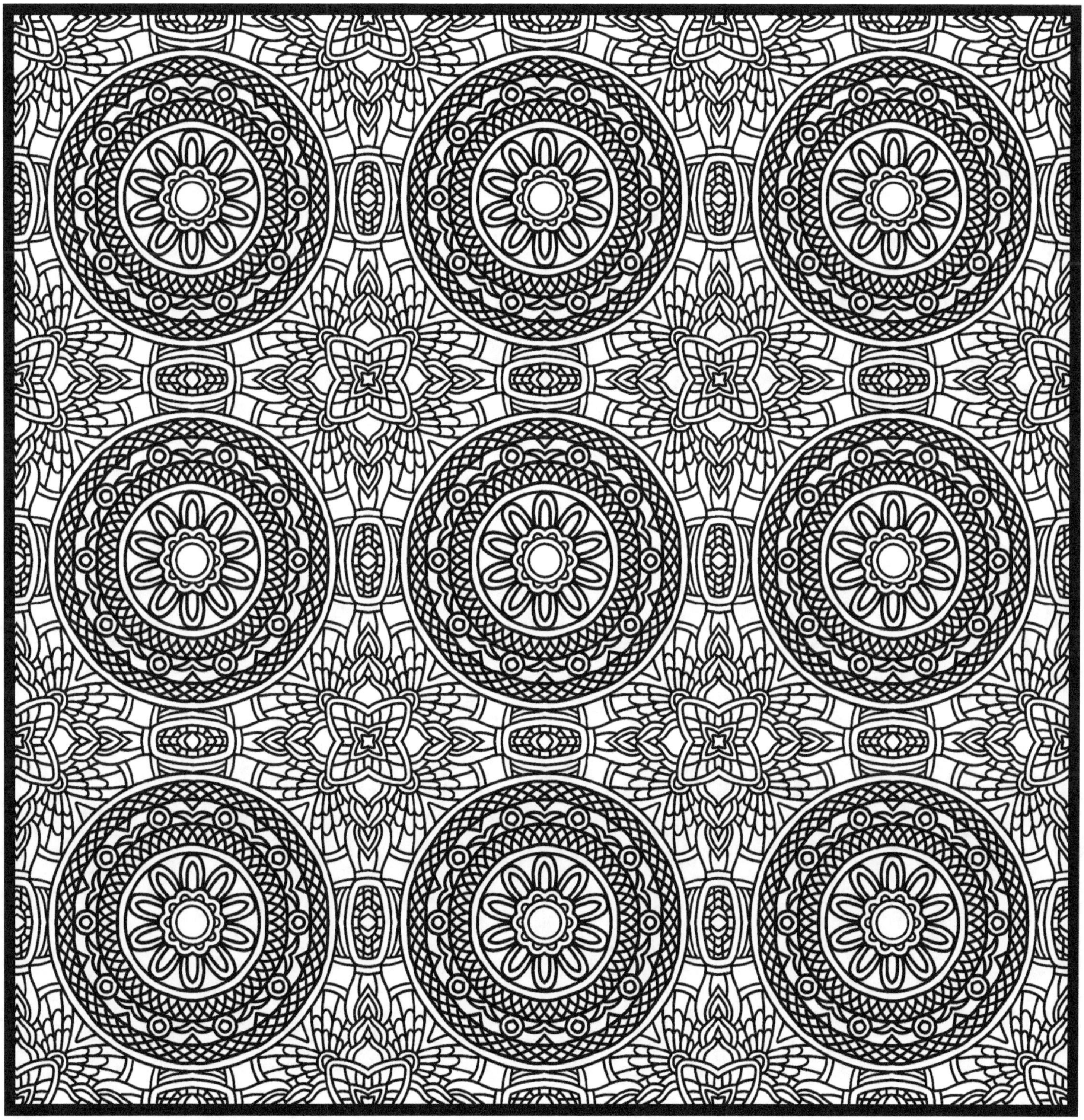

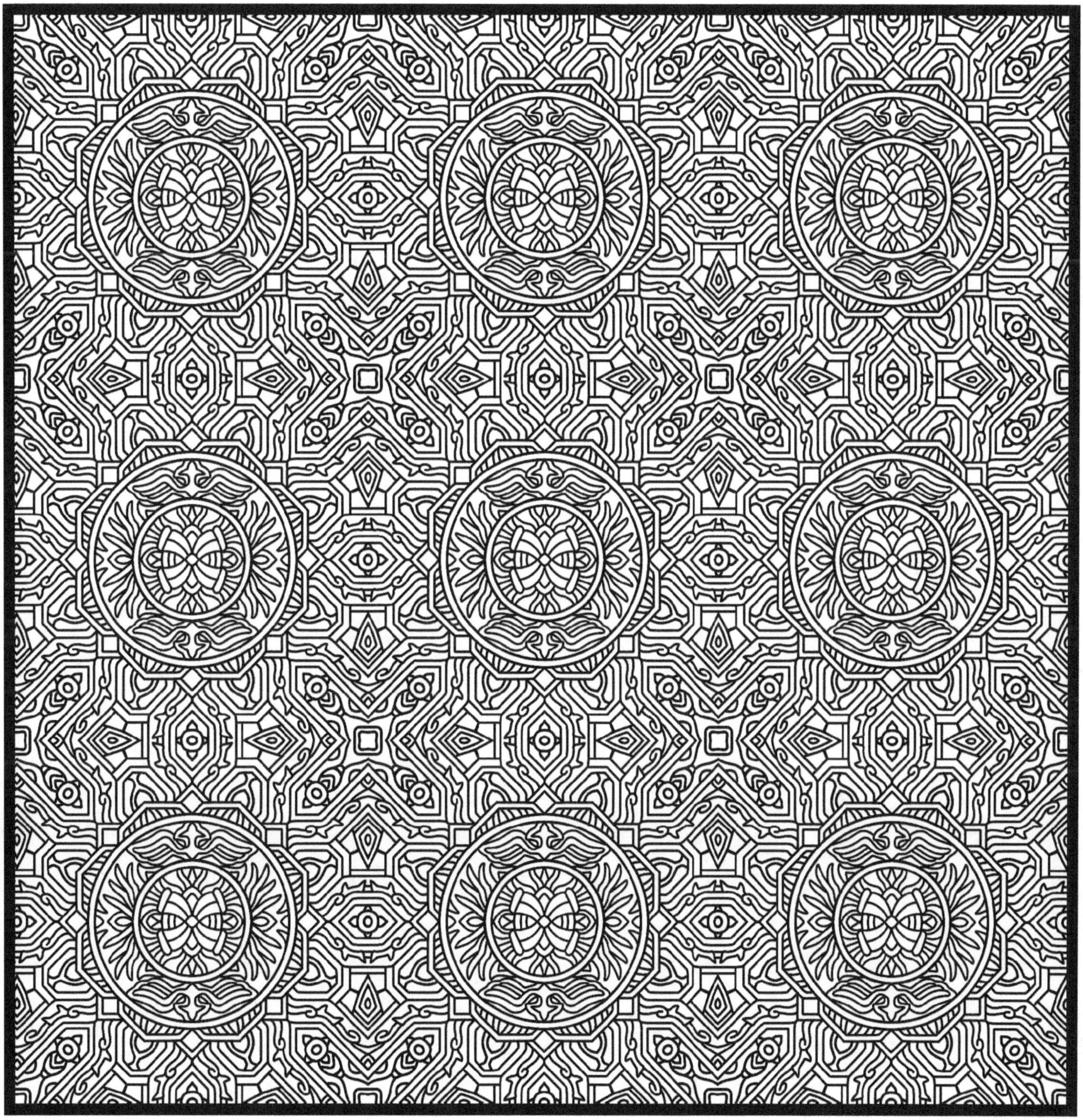

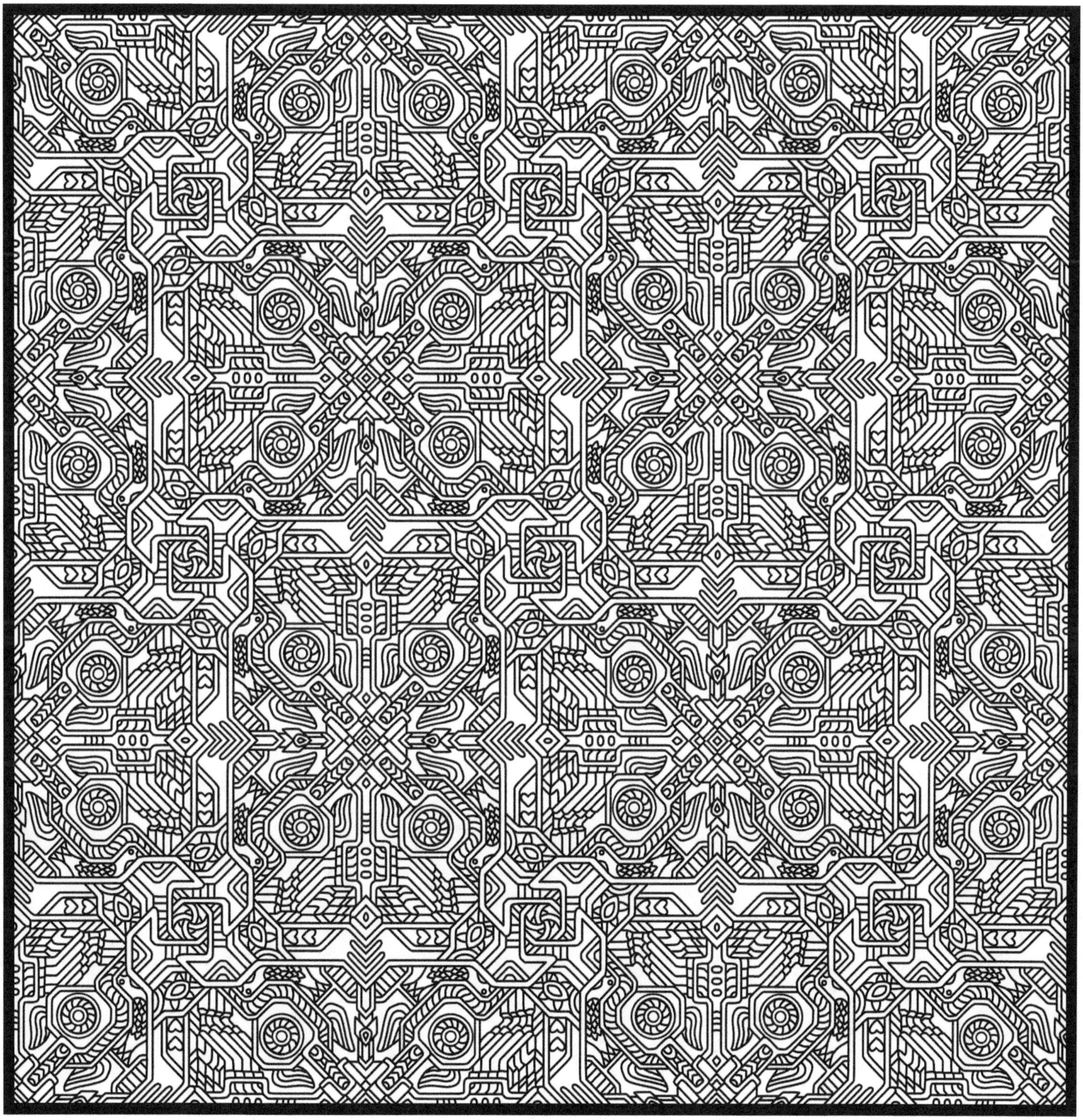

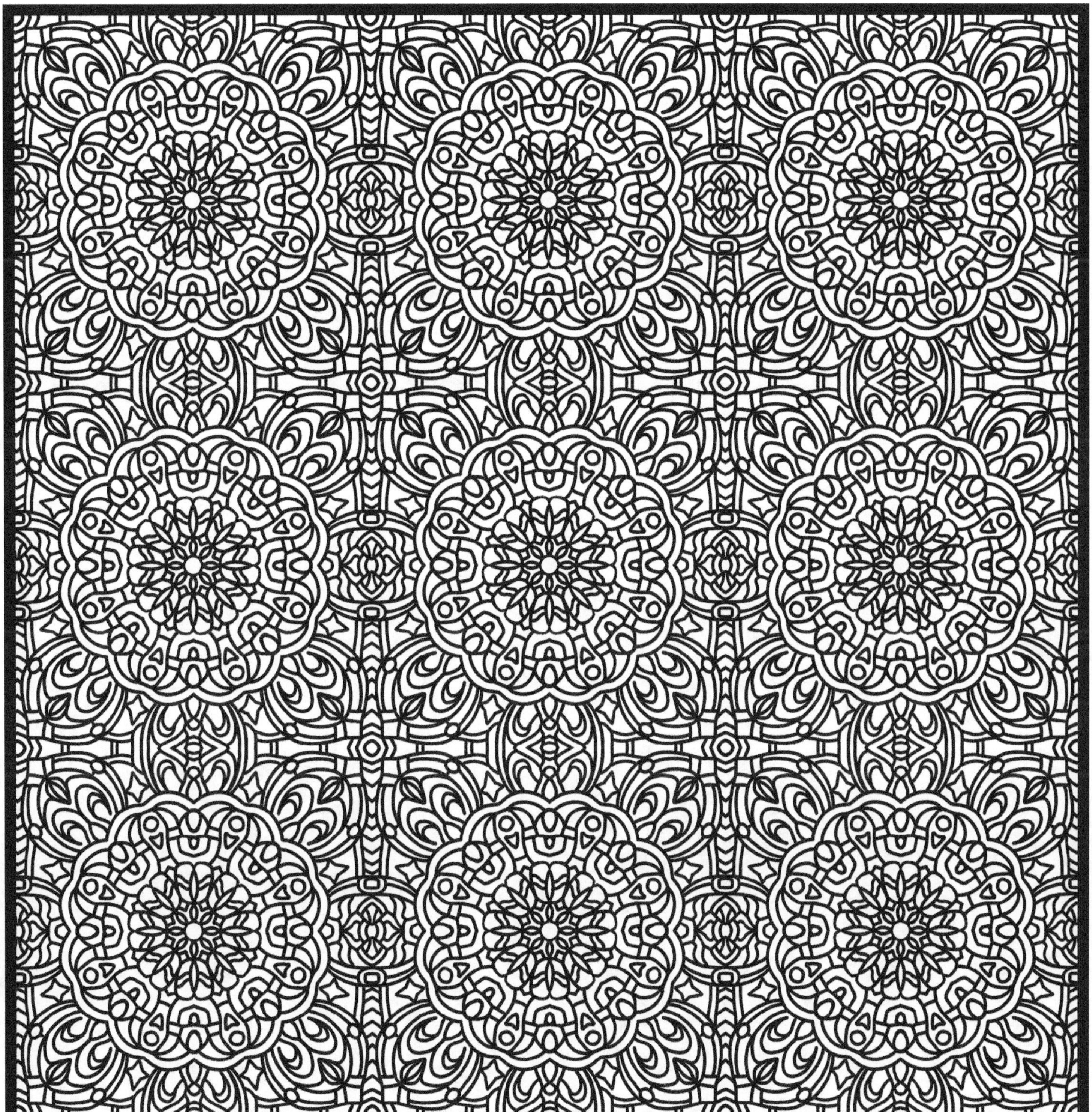

www.ingramcontent.com/pod-product-compliance
Lightning Source LLC
Chambersburg PA
CBHW080652180526
45168CB00008B/3390
* 9 7 8 1 5 0 8 6 5 4 4 4 5 *